Open the Door
to Better Communication
with Your Teen

The Family Movie Night
Prescription

David Garrison, M.D.

Open the Door to Better Communication with Your Teen

The Family Movie Night Prescription

David Garrison, M.D.

Love and Logic® INSTITUTE, Inc.
800-338-4065 • www.loveandlogic.com

Love and Logic Institute, Inc.

2207 Jackson Street, Golden, CO 80401-2300

www.loveandlogic.com

800-338-4065

LOVE AND LOGIC, LOVE & LOGIC, BECOMING A LOVE AND LOGIC PARENT, AMERICA'S PARENTING EXPERTS, LOVE AND LOGIC MAGIC, 9 ESSENTIAL SKILLS FOR THE LOVE AND LOGIC CLASSROOM, and are registered trademarks or trademarks of the Institute For Professional Development, Ltd. and may not be used without written permission expressly granted from the Institute For Professional Development, Ltd.

Movie Photos used with permission from Picture-Desk.

Library of Congress Cataloging-in-Publication Data

Garrison, David, 1970-
Open the door to better communication with your teen : the family movie
night prescription / David Garrison.
        p. cm.
Includes bibliographical references and index.
ISBN 978-1-935326-00-7 (pbk.)
1. Communication in the family--United States. 2. Parent and
teenager--United States. 3. Family--United States. 4. Motion pictures and
teenagers--United States. 5. Motion pictures and youth--United States. I.
Title.
HQ536.G356 2008
306.8740973--dc22
                            2008042744

Published and printed in the United States of America

Table of Contents

A Note to Readers vii

Introduction ix

Family Movie Night Instructions xvii

A League of Their Own 1

October Sky 5

The Insider 9

Erin Brockovich 13

Thirteen Days 17

Rabbit-Proof Fence 21

Iron Jawed Angels 25

Something the Lord Made 29

Hotel Rwanda 33

The Pursuit of Happyness 37

Freedom Writers 41

The Great Debaters 45

Making the Best of Media 49

Suggested Media Discussion Questions 51

Index of Discussion Questions 53

References 58

About the Author 64

A Note to Readers

This book is for parents and teens looking to be sure that they will always have open doors of communication. As a practical self-help tool, it can help open and keep open the doors of communication for many families. But when the door is slammed shut and won't open, this book should never be used as a substitute for formal mental health evaluation and treatment. Whenever parents have any concerns about the functioning or safety of their teen, they should always seek professional guidance. The following resources may be helpful to parents considering where to turn:

- **Primary Care Doctor**
  Whenever teens are struggling with any emotional or behavioral problems, the pediatrician or family practitioner should always be contacted. They are an invaluable resource, able to provide support and manage many problems and also help make appropriate referrals to other professionals when needed.

- **American Academy of Child and Adolescent Psychiatry**
  www.aacap.org
  A national organization for child and adolescent psychiatrists, AACAP has excellent resources for parents and teens, including brief "Facts for Families" about common disorders and dilemmas.

- **Mental Health America**
  www.nmha.org
  A national organization with links to local mental health associations, Mental Health America is also an excellent resource for mental health information and especially local support groups and professionals.

- **Love and Logic Institute**
  www.loveandlogic.com
  A parenting and educational philosophy that teaches empathy and support along with independence and natural consequences to allow youths to become responsible and well-adjusted adults.

This book is dedicated to my mom,
who would never stop believing in me.
You have been the inspiration for my belief in the
dreams and possibilities of every person,
especially the teenager.

Introduction

It was 11 o'clock on Sunday morning. Ashley finally emerged from her bedroom and went downstairs to the kitchen, where her parents were waiting. She did her best to act like everything was normal.

"Aren't you going to tell us what happened?" her mother asked.

Silence. Not even eye contact. Ashley poured herself some cereal and sat down at the kitchen table.

"You better believe that you're grounded for this," her father declared.

Still no response. Ashley just stared down at her cereal, tuned out.

"Do you know what it was like to be up worrying about you?" her mother began to lecture. "How could you break our trust like this? I feel like this isn't even you, like this is someone else's kid. What happened last night, Ashley? You have to tell us what's going on with you. What is the matter with you? Talk to us, Ashley. You just sit there and say nothing."

Ashley finally looked up from her cereal, now more than alert. Her eyes were teary, but her words came out like bullets.

"Why should I talk? You never listen."

She shoved her cereal bowl across the table and stormed back to her room, slamming the door enough to make her parents flinch.

Any parent and teen knows how quickly communication can break down in the heat of the moment. The everyday pressures that teens face can throw just about any family into a door-slamming meltdown like Ashley's. Teens start to imagine that their parents would never understand what it's like to be in their shoes. Meanwhile, parents try to get their teen to open up, only to be shut out the harder they try. Some parents may start to feel like good communication just isn't a possibility with teens. It can even be tempting for some parents and teens to convince themselves that their relationship just isn't as important as it used to be.

But the truth is that teens like Ashley never stop needing the support and guidance of their parents. Teens need to feel that they can come to their parents with anything. They need to know that their parents will be there for them no matter what the situation is. These open doors of communication are critical to make sure that parents are not left in the dark to worry about what may be happening. More importantly, they are essential to make sure parents and teens don't start to shut each other out and give up on their relationship.

This book is for any family looking for some assurance that they can talk about anything their teen is facing. It is not a traditional parenting book, with chapter after chapter of theory for parents to read on their own. More than anything, this guide is something for parents to do with their teens. Part workbook and part family game, it is a simple and unique way for parents to directly experience better communication with their teen.

As a child and adolescent psychiatrist working with troubled teens, I first developed the family movie night approach at the University of Rochester Medical Center. By capturing a family's attention and taking the focus away from their own conflicts, I have seen movies open the door to better communication in even the most stressed families. This book adapts the method and makes it a prescription for all families with teens. For families too over-scheduled to find enough time to spend together, the movies are an engaging common ground to get parents and teens in the same room. Even for families like Ashley's who may be too frustrated to want to spend time together, the movies are a non-intrusive and non-threatening conversation starter to begin the process of improving communication. The movies set the stage, allowing parents and teens to talk about difficult issues that are often too touchy to bring up directly.

In adapting the family movie night approach for all families, it was important to come up with a common theme that would be important for all parents and teens. The common feature of an inspiring and true story adds this extra element to capture the attention of all families. Each of the twelve movies tells the story of real people (based in history or current events) rising to the occasion to fight through adversity. With additional background information, families can learn more about the positive message in each person's story. In addition, their inspiring stories lead to conversation in two areas that are important for all families with teens: role models and strengths.

By finding their path through adversity, people like Homer Hickam of *October Sky*, Chris Gardner of *The Pursuit of Happyness* and Erin Brockovich make great role models for families. Teens in particular will identify with these and the other true underdog stories in each family movie night. After seeing them struggle and succeed in the movie, parents and teens can apply their story to their own lives. They can reflect on their own experience of success through adversity. They can also consider whether the true story is a good role model for their current life situation. For parents like Ashley's, desperate to know what kind of influences have a hold on their teen, the chance to have a discussion about role models is of immense value. It is a chance to explore what kind of role models teens are drawn to. It is also a chance to learn more about the guiding influences facing teens (and parents), out in the open.

The added emphasis on strengths is another key feature of each family movie night. Using the inspiring and true stories as a springboard, families can explore and appreciate their own strengths in themselves and each other. In each discussion, families are asked questions to explore past successes and future possibilities in their own lives. This extra focus on strengths in each family movie night also makes communication about problems easier. Feeling appreciated, teens like Ashley (and her parents) are less likely to shut down or blow up when they have to talk about problems. They have more confidence to be honest and communicate about difficult issues openly.

As we will see with Ashley's family, the way family movie nights open the doors of communication most of all is by giving families repeated chances to practice the way they talk to each other. The more practice they get, the easier it is for families to communicate when they are under stress. Knowing they can talk about difficult issues, families like Ashley's can feel confident that they are doing something to prevent problems before they get out of hand. Instead of an escalating crisis, issues like Ashley's mystery Saturday night become just another challenge to work through together.

Ashley was hesitant to try a family movie night but did eventually agree once she got to pick the first movie. Her parents thought it very fitting that she chose *Iron Jawed Angels*, the story of the rebellious young woman (Alice Paul) fighting for the woman's right to vote. It had been a while since they had all watched a movie together. But with some popcorn and pajamas (their movie ritual from years ago), they relaxed and really got into the story. After the movie was over, they read the *Background* and *Where to Learn More* sections. They each wondered what it would have been like to fight for a cause that seems so obvious by today's standards. Ashley wondered what the suffragists would be fighting for today.

Initially it didn't seem natural to stick around after the movie for a family discussion. Their instincts were to break off in different directions and leave the story behind them. But with their interest captured and some more popcorn, they agreed to try the discussion. They each took turns answering the Ten *Discussion Questions*. The questions started with less personal issues about the movie and then turned toward issues that were closer to home. They could all agree that Alice Paul was a great role model. Her stubborn determination to fight for a cause and get her way put Ashley's insistence on pushing the limits of her independence in a somewhat different light. The questions gave them all a chance to talk about these and other challenging issues through the movie. Things they had been afraid to talk about became more accessible.

Now that the movie had engaged Ashley's family in a spirited discussion, there was also the opportunity to "play" family movie night as a kind of communication game. They reviewed the two simple rules before beginning. First, listening as the first goal of communication. Second, agreeing to disagree when conflicts escalate. Both of these rules could be enforced in the movie discussion to provide direct feedback to each other where communication was breaking down.

The first rule was the hardest for Ashley's mom. She was surprised to find out how hard it was to just sit back and listen without inserting her own opinions. Like many parents, her instinct was to jump in to try to fix problems or teach lessons rather than first taking the time to understand where Ashley was coming from. No matter how good her intentions, her annoying habit of always having the right answers did nothing to help Ashley open up and express her own opinions. As a "family game," the movie discussion gave them all a chance to give direct feedback to each other on their listening. At any point in the discussion, they could put each other on the "hot seat" to make each other prove that each had understood where they were coming from.

The second communication rule, the ability to agree to disagree, was more challenging for Ashley's dad. As in many families, there was an ongoing debate in Ashley's family about who was the most stubborn. Over any little thing, they both wanted desperately to convince each other that they were right and the other was wrong. Of course this only caused them each to dig in and hold onto their position more. An even bigger problem was that they could get so frustrated with each other over their disagreements that they could shut each other out altogether. For Ashley and her dad, the movie discussion gave them each a chance to practice backing away from these conflicts. As a "family game," when they played the "agree to disagree" card, they could send each other the message that they could and would stick together no matter how big their disagreements were.

Two Essential Communication Rules With Teens

1. Listening: when someone feels that they were not understood, they can put anybody on the "hot seat" to make them prove that they were listening.

2. Agreeing to Disagree: when someone feels understood but disagreements continue, this "card" can be played by anyone to de-escalate the conflict.

The Iron Jawed Angels discussion gave Ashley and her parents several chances to work on the art of both listening and disagreement. Taking the extra time to listen first before anything else gave them each the confidence that they were understood by each other.

Once they got the hang of listening to each other, they discovered that they were less likely to find themselves in disagreement. When there was disagreement, they were better able to respect their different opinions and let things go. Of course, this was much easier when it was a small matter. When Ashley complained that her parents didn't trust her and that her curfew was unfair, they had a much harder time letting that one go.

After one family movie night, it was clear that Ashley and her parents still hadn't worked through all their problems, especially the problem of trust. Without more communication, this trust problem could have easily spiraled out of control. Ashley could have protested more and more angrily, causing her parents to fight back with more rules and expectations. While they would see their rules as protection, Ashley would take this lack of trust as a personal insult. She would see her parents' worries as anger and judgment. This lack of trust would be a reminder that she had disappointed her parents and that they lost their faith in her.

Not about to give up, Ashley and her parents decided to try more family movie nights. What they discovered was that the secret to rebuilding trust was above all to just keep communicating. Now that they were better able to listen and agree to disagree, it was much easier to talk about those touchy subjects that had been too risky to bring up before. With their foot in the door, they were gradually able to talk about more personal issues with greater success. This gave Ashley's parents the confidence that they knew where she was coming from on the issues they were most worried about.

The added communication in each family discussion about role models and strengths also helped them regain their confidence in each other. The more they talked about role models, the more Ashley's parents felt like they knew what her overall sense of direction was. The more they talked about each others' strengths, the less defensive they were and the more Ashley felt like she could be honest about anything. All of this allowed them to finally start trusting each other again. With more trust, they could compromise with each other more easily and there was much less to disagree about.

After several movies, Ashley's parents began to see another important lesson in communicating with teens. They realized that the point of their communication with Ashley was never to simply tell her what to think. They couldn't force her to believe what they believed or to act as they acted. There was no lecture that was going to give her a sense of responsibility. But what open communication could do was allow them to be present for Ashley, so that they didn't miss the chance to help her work through important issues. By focusing on listening and agreeing to disagree, the movie discussions helped them nurture Ashley's ability to think and make decisions for herself. As described in Love and Logic, they were there for her as "consultant parents," allowing her to take and learn responsibility through her own thinking.

Ashley did tell her parents why she came home late that night. There were also several other things they found out about each other that they never knew. With each family movie night, their confidence grew that the doors of communication were open and would remain open. Now that Ashley felt like her parents understood her and believed in her, she was much more comfortable talking with her parents about anything. Now that they all felt like they could disagree without it blowing up, they felt more comfortable taking on even the touchiest subjects. With each family movie night, their confidence grew in their ability to communicate with each other, no matter how stressful the situation. Not only this, they also felt reassured that they had taken action to be sure that their relationship most definitely still mattered.

Family Movie Night Instructions

The Movie: The youngest person is given the chance to select the first movie. An exact time for the movie should be set. Parents and teens should watch the movie together even if someone has already seen the movie before. Siblings, extended family or friends may also be included depending on their ages and family preference.

Hints For Scheduling Family Movie Nights

1. Busy and conflicting schedules may make it unrealistic for the entire family to participate in each family movie night. Families should consider including just one teen (or one parent) at a time rather than waiting for schedules to align.

2. The best time for the family discussion is right after the movie ends. The chances of having a good discussion are much lower if families wait and try to schedule for a later time.

The Background: Immediately after the movie, someone reads aloud the Beyond the Movie and Where to Learn More sections. This is also the best time to pop the popcorn (or any other family movie ritual) to make sure everyone sticks around for the family discussion.

The Discussion: Parents and teens take turns answering the ten Discussion Questions. There should be no pressure to finish all the questions. Quieter family members may be given the option of reviewing the questions first and choosing the five questions they would feel most comfortable answering. Families may choose to spend more time on a particular question or improvise a new direction to the discussion. Families may also choose to set a one-hour time limit for the discussion or continue the discussion at a later time.

Communication Rules: Before the discussion, parents and teens should review the two communication rules to practice in each family movie night:

Two Essential Communication Rules With Teens

1. Listening: when someone feels that they were not understood, they can put anybody on the "hot seat" to make them prove that they were listening.

2. Agreeing to Disagree: when someone feels understood but disagreements continue, this "card" may be played by anyone to de-escalate the conflict.

A League of Their Own (1992)

PG for language
128 minutes

The Story of the AAGPBL

This movie portrays the first season of the All-American Girls Professional Baseball League. It is like many down-to-the-wire sports
movies, but with the central theme of gender equality as its back-
drop. Showing how rigid cultural expectations were for women in
the 1940s, A League of Their Own highlights for women just how
far they have come (as well as how much further there is to go).
There are also interesting subplots of sibling rivalry and alcoholism.

Beyond the Movie

- The All-American Girls Professional Baseball League (AAGPBL) had twelve seasons from 1943 to 1954 and at one point even drew more fans than men's Major League Baseball (MLB). The Rockford Peaches were the dominant team in the league, winning the championship in 1945, 1948, 1949, and 1950. As in the movie, an exhibit at the MLB Hall of Fame paying tribute to the women of the AAGPBL was opened in 1988.

- The makers of A League of Their Own insist all characters in the movie are fictional. However, the manager Jimmy Dugan (played by Tom Hanks) is very similar to Hall of Famer Jimmie Foxx. Like Dugan, Foxx once hit 58 home runs in a season, was known for his drinking, and was also a manager in the AAGPBL.

- League developer Philip Wrigley (of chewing gum fame rather not chocolate bars) tried very hard to promote the league with traditional "feminine" appearances. All AAGPBL players were required to have chaperones, take etiquette classes, and keep a league regulation "beauty kit."

- In 1931, the AA team Chattanooga Lookouts signed 17-year-old Jackie Mitchell, who would become famous for striking out Babe Ruth and Lou Gerhig in an exhibition game. Embarrassed by his performance, Babe Ruth threw his bat after a called strike three. Not to be outdone, the commissioner of MLB voided her contract a few days later. He claimed that baseball is too strenuous for a woman.

- Opportunity for women to play sports changed dramatically with the passing of Title IX in 1972. Title IX required colleges to give men and women the same opportunities in both academics and athletics. Over the next three decades, the number of women in college sports went from 29,977 to 155,513. During this same time, the number of high school girls playing varsity sports went from 294,015 to 2,806,998.

Where to Learn More

BOOKS

- Blumenthal, Karen. *Let Me Play: The Story of Title IX: The Law That Changed The Future of Girls in America.* Atheneum, 2005.

- Johnson, Susan. *When Women Played Hardball.* Seal Press, 1994.

- Macy, Sue. *A Whole New Ball Game: The Story of the All-American Girls Professional Baseball League.* Puffin, 1995.

DOCUMENTARIES

- *A League of Their Own – The Documentary* (1986). Sony Pictures, 1994.

WEBSITES

- Official Website of the All-American Girls Professional Baseball League: www.aagpbl.org

Discussion Questions

1. Does your athletic ability come more by nature or by hard work? What is your best sport and/or your best athletic performance?

2. Do you think there are gender stereotypes for men and women today? Have you ever felt like your options were limited because of your gender?

3. In you were in Dottie's place, would you have put marriage before baseball? Why or why not?

4. Do you think "All The Way" May was too openly sexual? Where does your family stand on sexual experimentation?

5. Why do you think Jimmy Dugan had a drinking problem? Where does your family stand on drinking?

6. When have you found yourself in a situation where you felt like a nag (like Dottie) or a mule (like Kit)? What about a time where you played the other role?

7. Why do you think Dottie and Kit were able to get past their sibling rivalry? When have you been able to work through a "rivalry"?

8. "There's no crying in baseball." When do you think crying should be avoided? When do you think it might be encouraged? When was the last time you cried?

9. In tears and on the verge of quitting, Kit was able to find the strength to get the winning hit and knockdown run. When was a time that you performed well under pressure? How about a time when you felt like quitting but persisted?

10. Do you think the Rockford Peaches are good role models for you? Why or why not?

October Sky (1999)

Rated PG for language, brief teen sensuality and alcohol use,
and for some thematic elements
108 minutes

The Story of Homer Hickam and the Rocket Boys

This is the story of four high school teens from a small coal-mining
town in West Virginia who fulfill their dreams of building a rocket
that is the surprise winner of the National Science Fair. The movie
also portrays complicated and heartfelt families ties, including the
love of a father played like a drill sergeant and the determination of
a teen to be true to himself.

Beyond the Movie

- After the Soviet Union launched Sputnik in 1957, the following year the United States established the National Aeronautics and Space Administration (NASA). Its first mission was the Mercury Program (to put humans into space) and is chronicled in the book and movie The Right Stuff. Its second mission was the Apollo Program (to put humans on the moon) and is depicted in the movie Apollo 13 and the documentary In the Shadow of the Moon.

- While in town buying a suit for the National Science Fair, Homer Hickam met Senator John F. Kennedy at a presidential campaign rally. To the cheers of the West Virginia coal minors, Hickam told JFK that the United States should go to the moon. One year later, JFK would make the Apollo Program a major focus of his presidency. The mission was accomplished in 1969 with Apollo 11.

- After serving in Vietnam, Hickam would work for NASA as an aerospace engineer from 1981-1999. An expert in spacecraft design and crew training, he worked closely on the Hubble Telescope and the International Space Station.

- Rocket Boys, the inspiration for October Sky, was published in 1998 and was a NY Times #1 bestseller. Hickam then wrote three follow-up memoirs. First was The Coalwood Way (which takes up Hickam's story in his senior year of high school). Next was Sky of Stone (where Hickam works in the mines during his summer vacation from college). Last was We Are Not Afraid (a tribute to the values and courage of Coalwood as a model for the country after the 9/11 attacks).

- Hickam went on to write many more books as well, including the novels Back to the Moon, Red Helmet and the Josh Thurlow series of novels about a WWII Coast Guard Captain. He is in contact and good friends with the remaining Coalwood Rocket Boys. Several of them, along with Hickam, are seen in the Rocket Boys Story and Aiming High interviews on the October Sky DVD Extras.

Where to Learn More

BOOKS

- Hickam, Homer. *Rocket Boys*. Delta, 2000.
- Hickam, Homer. *The Coalwood Way*. Island Books; 1st Ed, 2001.
- Hickam, Homer. *Sky of Stone*. Dell, 2002.
- Hickam, Homer. *We Are Not Afraid*. We Are HCI, 2002.

DOCUMENTARIES

- *In the Shadow of the Moon* (2007). Velocity/Thinkfilm, 2008.

WEBSITES

- www.HomerHickam.com

Discussion Questions

1. If you could get a full scholarship anywhere you wanted, where would you go? What would you study?

2. How did Miss Riley help Homer reach his dream? Who has been your greatest mentor?

3. Why did Homer say he couldn't give up on his dream? When have you been the most determined not to give up?

4. What qualities do you think are more attractive to the opposite sex, brains like Homer or brawn like his brother Jim?

5. Would you have gone to work in the coalmines to support your family if you had been in Homer's shoes? Why or why not?

6. What did you most admire about Homer's dad? What is something you appreciate about your dad?

7. What did you most admire about Homer's mom? What is something you appreciate about your mom?

8. When do you think Homer's dad was most proud of him? For parents, when have you been most proud of your teen? For teens, when would you be most proud if you were a parent?

9. How did Homer finally convince his dad to come see his rocket launch? What is something you would want your parent see you do?

10. Do you think Homer Hickam is a good role model for you? Why or why not?

The Insider (1999)

Rated R for language
157 minutes

The Story of Jeffrey Wigand and Lowell Bergman

This is the courageous story of tobacco insider Jeffrey Wigand who stands up to the lies of Big Tobacco with the encouragement of 60 Minutes producer Lowell Bergman. The Insider shows how hard it can be to speak up for the truth. Starting with the dangers of cigarettes, the movie is an opening for families to talk about the dangers of any addictive substance.

Beyond the Movie

- The Master Settlement Agreement (MSA) of 1998 was the largest civil settlement in United States history. It required tobacco companies to pay $246 billion to the states for past Medicaid expenses of tobacco related illnesses. As a condition of the settlement, Brown and Williamson dropped their charges against Jeffrey Wigand for breaking his confidentiality agreement when he spoke on 60 Minutes.

- In 2007, the amount the tobacco industry spent on marketing was more than 1800% what the states spent on tobacco prevention. Although the MSA outlawed the use of youth oriented advertising such as Joe Camel, one study showed that magazine advertisements reach more than 80% of high school students an average of 17 times a year.

- In the 1980s, the tobacco industry tried to suppress the documentary Death in the West. It is the story of six original Marlboro Men, five of them with lung cancer and one with emphysema. The film shows each cowboy riding horses then and now (one with an oxygen tank), mixed with interviews of Phillip Morris executives saying that nobody really knows if cigarettes cause cancer. This perspective is portrayed more comically in the 2006 movie, Thank You For Smoking.

- According to the Centers for Disease Control (CDC), smoking shortens the average lifespan by 14 years.

- According to the 2006 National Survey on Drug Use and Health, smokers are more than 400% likely than non-smokers to use illegal drugs or drink heavily.

- After winning a national teacher of the year award in 1996, Jeffrey Wigand became a national spokesperson for the dangers of tobacco use and founder of Smoke-Free Kids, Inc. He is featured in numerous documentaries and an educational DVD Secrets Through the Smoke that is available at no cost from the CDC.

• After the release of The Insider, Lowell Bergman left 60 Minutes in the midst of criticism from Mike Wallace and producer Dan Hewitt of their negative portrayal in the movie. He became a producer for PBS's Frontline and won a Pulitzer Prize in 2004 for A Dangerous Business, a story of injuries in the workplace. In 2007 he co-produced News War, a documentary about the media in the modern age. He also continued teaching investigative reporting at the University of California at Berkley.

Where to Learn More

DOCUMENTARIES

• *Secrets Through the Smoke*. CDC, 2001.

• *Death in the West* (1983). Pyramid Home Video, 1991.

• *Frontline: News War*. The Complete Series. PBS, 2007.

WEBSITES

• www.JeffreyWigand.com

• www.thetruth.com

• www.tobacoofreekids.org

Discussion Questions

1. If it were up to you, how would you spend the $246 billion (nearly $1,000 per American) the tobacco industry was made to pay the government for tobacco related Medicaid expenses?

2. Where do you think the tobacco industry will be in 20 years? How about 100 years?

3. What are the factors that keep people smoking? If you smoke, why do you do it?

4. Why do you think teenage smoking is associated with such large increases in illegal drug use and heavy alcohol use?

5. Where do you and your family stand on the issue of other addictive substances?

6. Would you have had the courage, to testify against Big Tobacco as Jeffrey Wigand did? Why or why not?

7. When have you had to show the courage to tell the truth when ignoring it was the easy thing to do? Or when were you close to telling a lie but stopped yourself?

8. How did Lowell Bergman help Jeffrey Wigand in his most difficult hour? When has someone helped you through a really difficult time?

9. Do you think Jeffrey Wigand is a good role model for you? Why or why not?

10. Do you think Lowell Bergman is a good role model for you? Why or why not?

Erin Brockovich (2000)

Rated R for language
130 minutes

The Story of Erin Brockovich

Originally billed as "Rocky in a miniskirt", this movie tells the story of a single mother who fearlessly stands up for a small town poisoned by a major corporation. Her determination and self-confidence in the face of adversity may inspire families and especially teens who like to stand up for the underdog. Her struggles balancing work and family, along with her provocative style, make for further discussion.

Beyond the Movie

- The 1996 settlement with PG&E for the record $333 million was controversial in the scientific community. Many doubted that Chromium 6 could be responsible for the ailments in the Hinkley residents since it was only known to cause cancer when inhaled. However, a 2007 National Institute of Health study sided against these critics. It concluded that Chromium 6 is carcinogenic to animals when ingested in water, as was the case in the contaminated Hinkley groundwater.

- Prior to production, Brockovich specifically identified Julia Roberts as the one person she didn't want to play her in the movie. But in the end she did praise Robert's Academy Award winning performance. Brockovich also made an appearance of her own, as the waitress in one of the opening scenes of the movie. She is also featured on the DVD Extras.

- Just after the movie's release, Brockovich's boyfriend (the biker boyfriend) and her first husband made an attempt at extortion. They threatened to tell the media that Brockovich was an unfit mother and that she had had a relationship with Ed Masry unless they were given $310,000. Brockovich and Masry alerted the authorities and both men were arrested in a sting operation.

- Brockovich really did remember the names and cases of all 634 Hinkley plaintiffs. She made a habit of memorizing as a way of coping with her life-long struggle with dyslexia. Brockovich also battled and overcame both panic disorder and anorexia.

- Brockovich went on to become an environmentalist and continue her legal consulting. In 2002, she published Take It From Me: Life's a Struggle But You Can Win. It is a more extended version of her life story that includes growing up and struggling as a single mom. In 2003 she became the host of a Lifetime program Final Justice, which told stories of other inspiring women overcoming adversity.

Where to Learn More

BOOKS

- Brockovich, Erin and Eliot, Marc. *Take It From Me: Life's a Struggle But You Can Win.* McGraw-Hill, 2002.

DOCUMENTARIES

- *American Justice: The Erin Brockovich Story.* A and E Home Video, 2001.

WEBSITES

- www.Brockovich.com

- Scorecard – The Pollution Information Site: www.scorecard.org

Discussion Questions

1. As judge, how much would you have made PG&E pay the Jensens and the other 634 Hinkley plaintiffs? Why?

2. What would you do with a $2 million bonus?

3. What is your favorite "David and Goliath" story of all time?

4. What is your opinion of Erin Brockovich's communication? With her kids? At the office? With the Hinkley plaintiffs?

5. What is your opinion of the way Erin Brockovich dressed? When have you disagreed with someone about how to dress?

6. Erin was in tears when she missed her daughter's first words. When have you missed something important in your family because you were so busy?

7. In the end, Erin's kids did appreciate her work even though she spent less time with them. When have you appreciated the hard work of a parent?

8. What made Erin Brockovich such a strong person? What experience have you gone through that has made you a stronger person?

9. How did Erin Brockovich improve her self-confidence? What experience has raised or would raise your self-confidence?

10. Do you think Erin Brockovich is a good role model for you? Why or why not?

Thirteen Days (2001)

Rated PG-13 for brief strong language
145 minutes

The Story of JFK and RFK in the Cuban Missile Crisis

This movie portrays two great leaders and brothers who succeeded at perhaps the greatest conflict resolution of all time, preventing nuclear war with the Soviet Union. Parents and teens can learn from their peacemaking skills and discuss how they resolve their own conflicts.

Beyond the Movie

- The Cuban Missile Crisis is widely believed to be the closest the world has ever been to nuclear war. For the only time in history, U.S. military forces were at DEFCON 2. (DEFCON 1 would be called if the U.S. were under immediate attack).

- Much of the dialogue for Thirteen Days was taken directly from transcripts of 23 hours of White House meetings that were secretly recorded by JFK and not released until 1996. The movie title comes from a memoir of the crisis that Robert F. Kennedy wrote in 1969.

- Kevin O'Donnell (played by Kevin Costner) had a much less prominent role in the crisis than portrayed in the movie. However, he was present in the inner circle meetings and was recorded to have one heated exchange with defense secretary Robert McNamara. McNamara would remain defense secretary into the Vietnam War and tell of his experience in the 2003 Academy Award winning documentary The Fog of War.

- JFK and RFK were the 2nd and 7th of 9 children. Their father was a wealthy banker and U.S. Ambassador to England with high political hopes for his children. His first son, Joseph Kennedy, was killed in a WWII mission to knock out Hitler's V-1 rockets. This left his dreams in the hands of JFK, who had survived a WWII attack by a Japanese destroyer. With his father's support, JFK became a congressman in 1946 and then a senator in 1952. In 1961, following a campaign led by his brother RFK, JFK became the youngest president of the United States at the age of 43.

- JFK's presidency lasted just 2 years as he was assassinated in 1963. Besides his leadership in the Cuban Missile Crisis, JFK was also known for his pledge to get to the moon and for the Peace Corps.

- As Attorney General, RFK played a key role in the fight for the groundbreaking Civil Rights Act of 1964. He went on to be Senator of New York before running for president in 1968. Just two months after the assassination of Martin Luther King Jr., RFK was assassinated after giving a victory speech for the California primary.

- The movies JFK and Bobby portray detailed (and very controversial in the case of JFK) accounts of the two Kennedy assassinations.

Where to Learn More

BOOKS

- Kennedy, Robert F. Thirteen Days: A Memoir of the Cuban Missile Crisis. W.W. Norton and Company, 1999.

- May, Ernest and Zelikow, Philip. The Kennedy Tapes: Inside the White House During the Cuban Missile Crisis. W.W. Norton and Company, 2002.

- Stern, Sheldon. The Week the World Stood Still: Inside the Secret Cuban Missile Crisis. Stanford University Press, 2004.

DOCUMENTARIES

- The Fog of War – Eleven Lessons From the Life of Robert S. McNamara. Sony Pictures, 2004.

- American Experience: The Kennedys. PBS DVD Video, 2003.

Discussion Questions

1. Do you think JFK or RFK would be good presidents today? Why or why not?

2. Would you ever want to be the president? Why or why not?

3. How did JFK feel pressured by military leaders to "abandon his own moral judgment?" When have you felt threatened by peer pressure to do something you felt was wrong?

4. Are you apt to come across as too hard or too soft when you are in conflict with others?

5. Throughout the crisis, RFK is the dealmaker who gets people on the same page. Who is like this in your family?

6. Faced with two letters from Krushchev, one a peace offering and the other a threat of escalation, the Kennedys are unsure which to respond to. RFK has the idea to simply ignore the second letter. When you are given mixed messages, peaceful and threatening, which are you more apt to respond to? Have you ever tried the RFK strategy?

7. Why do you think the Cuban Missile Crisis ended peacefully?

8. When was a time that your family made it through a crisis of escalating conflict?

9. What would your family do tonight if the president of the United States announced that the country was at DEFCON 1?

10. Do you think JFK or RFK are good role models for you? Why or why not?

Rabbit-Proof Fence (2002)

Rated PG for emotional thematic material
94 minutes

The Story of Molly Craig and the Stolen Generation

Among the many thousands of Aborigine children stolen from their parents by the Australian government, the three determined girls portrayed in this movie break free and walk an incredible 1500 miles along a rabbit-proof fence to get back home to their family. This amazing story of children going to such extraordinary lengths to get home can put the importance of family in perspective. Families can talk about their own experiences with separation and consider what keeps them attached.

Beyond the Movie

- Between 1869 and 1969, somewhere between one in three and one in ten Aborigines – an estimated 100,000 children – were taken away from their families and placed in various institutions. They have been called the Stolen Generation.

- Gracie was captured as seen in the movie and transported back to Moore River where she completed her education. She married, had six children and passed away in 1983, never to return to Jigalong.

- After making it back to Jigalong, Daisy was able to stay and make her home there for the rest of her life. She married and had four children.

- Molly Craig was brought back to Moore River nine years later with her two daughters, Annabelle and Doris. One year later, she carried her 18-month-old daughter Annabelle on her back the 1600 kilometers all the way back to Jigalong again. Annabelle was taken away from Molly again and brought back to Moore River at age three. They would never see each other again. Molly remained in Jigalong until she died in 2004 at the age of 86.

- Molly was eventually reunited with her older daughter, Doris. When they met, Doris didn't speak her native language and believed that her mother had abandoned her (a common belief among the Stolen Generation). But Doris would reclaim her family, reconnecting with her mother and learning the stories of their past. She went on to write a trilogy documenting three generations of her family. First she wrote, Caprice: A Stockman's Daughter (1990), a story of Molly's mom. Then she wrote the story of Molly, Daisy and Gracie, Follow the Rabbit-Proof Fence (1996), which has been translated into 11 languages. Finally she wrote, Under the Wintamarra Tree (2002), Doris' own story.

Where to Learn More

BOOKS

- Pilkington, Doris. *Follow the Rabbit-Proof Fence.* University of Queensland Press, 1996.

- Pilkington, Doris. *Caprice: A Stockman's Daughter.* University of Queensland Press, 1990.

- Pilkington, Doris. *Under the Wintamarra Tree.* University of Queensland Press, 2002.

- Arden, Harvey. *Dreamkeepers: A Spirit-Journey into Aboriginal Australia.* Harper Perennial, 1995.

DOCUMENTARIES

- *Ancient Mysteries: Dreamtime of the Aborigines.* A and E Home Video, 1997.

WEBSITES

- Human Rights and Equal Opportunity Commission (an Australian government human rights agency). www.hreoc.gov.au

Discussion Questions

1. What would your policy have been for the biracial Australians if you were Chief Protector of the Aborigines?

2. Do you think the Jigalong people have anything important to teach mainstream culture? Like what?

3. How do you think rituals are important to the Jigalong people? What rituals are important to your family?

4. Whose side do you think Tracker was on, that of Australian officials or the Aborigines? When have you ever felt stuck between two worlds, with different values and expectations pressuring you in different directions?

5. If you were forced to "go walkabout," how far and for how long do you think you could survive? Who would you want alongside you on your journey and why?

6. Compared to Molly and Daisy's mother, how would you express your grief if your kids were taken away from you?

7. Had you been in Gracie's shoes, would you have stayed with Molly and Daisy or gone your own way to find your mother in Wilunda? Why?

8. What is the longest and farthest you've ever been away from your family? How did you cope?

9. If you were forcibly separated from your family, what would give you the strength to escape back home?

10. Do you think Molly Craig is a good role model for you? Why or why not?

Iron Jawed Angels (2004)

Not Rated
123 minutes

The Story of Alice Paul and the Suffragists

This movie should appeal to anyone with a rebellious and activist spirit. Iron Jawed Angels shows Alice Paul and her followers engage in civil disobedience and even a hunger strike to finally win a constitutional amendment to give women the right to vote. Their story can open a discussion of parents' and teens' own experiences with rebellion, both with and without cause.

Beyond the Movie

- There have been three amendments to the U.S. Constitution on the right to vote. The first was the 15th Amendment, giving the vote to men regardless of race. The second was the 19th Amendment, giving the vote to women. Last was the 26th Amendment, expanding the voting age to 18 and up.

- Suffragists (fighting for the right to vote) and abolitionists (fighting to end slavery) worked side by side in the mid 1800s. In Rochester, New York, Susan B. Anthony formed a close relationship with the leading abolitionist, Frederick Douglas. After the Civil War in 1865, Anthony and Elizabeth Cady Stanton wanted the 15th Amendment to give the vote to women as well as African Americans. Anthony and Cady continued to fight for women's suffrage but only won the right to vote in a few states, beginning with Wyoming in 1890.

- Before they joined the suffrage movement in the United States, Alice Paul met Lucy Burns met in England where the suffragists were much more militant. Their tactics included heckling, rock throwing, and window smashing to draw attention to their cause. In one protest, Alice Paul said she personally smashed 48 windows.

- November 15, 1917 at the Occaquan Workhouse was called the "Night of Terror." On that night 40 guards brutally attacked 33 imprisoned suffragists with clubs. It would prove to be a very powerful demonstration of civil disobedience. Like Ghandi (as portrayed in the Academy Award winning film Ghandi) and James Farmer, Jr. (as portrayed in The Great Debaters), the suffragists would win popular support by their defiance.

- Alice Paul never married and devoted herself to the woman's rights movement her entire life. In 1923, she was the original author of the Equal Rights Amendment. Its aim was to give equal legal rights to all citizens, regardless of gender. In 1972, the amendment was finally passed by Congress, but never passed in the required three-quarters states. Alice Paul died at the age of 92 in 1977.

Where to Learn More

BOOKS

- Baker, Jean. *Sisters: The Lives of America's Suffragists*. Hill and Wang, 2006.

- Bausam, Ann. *With Courage and Cloth: Winning the Fight for a Women's Right to Vote*. National Geographic Children's Books, 2004.

DOCUMENTARIES

- *One Woman, One Vote*. PBS Home Video, 1996.

- *Not for Ourselves Alone: The Story of Stanton and Anthony*. PBS Home Video, 1999.

WEBSITES

- www.alicepaul.org

- www.equalrightsamendment.org

Discussion Questions

1. What impact do you think the 19th Amendment has had? How do you think the world might be different if women had more political power than they do now?

2. At what age do you think people should have the right to vote? Why?

3. Alice Paul said she did once wish she were a boy when she saw her brother peeing in the snow. Would you ever change places with the opposite sex for a while? Why or why not?

4. Alice Paul did pee in an English Lord's boot. What is the boldest prank you ever took part in?

5. Do you think Alice Paul would have accomplished less if she had married Ben Weisman? When have you found the best balance of work and family?

6. When Inez Millholland died, Alice Paul was paralyzed with guilt. Tell the story of a time that you felt guilty.

7. What rebellious thing have you ever done for no good reason?

8. What rebellious thing have you ever done that was for a good reason? What was the reason?

9. Is there a modern cause that would send you to a protest? Could you imagine any cause that you would go to jail or on a hunger strike for?

10. Do you think Alice Paul is a good role model for you? Why or why not?

Something the Lord Made (2004)

Not Rated
110 minutes

The Story of Vivien Thomas and Alfred Blalock

This movie portrays a prominent surgeon and his underappreciated African American assistant performing the world's first successful heart surgery. It is a story of cutting edge medicine and civil rights, as Vivien Thomas goes unrecognized for years despite his achievements that would pave the way for modern heart surgery. Something the Lord Made should capture the attention of any family curious about medicine and passionately against discrimination.

Beyond the Movie

- The Blalock-Taussig shunt (or Thomas-Blalock-Taussig shunt, as has recently been suggested) was an exceptionally difficult procedure to perform. On the website for the PBS documentary Partners of the Heart, there is a description of the procedure, including an interactive version to perform a virtual operation.

- While Alfred Blalock was the scientist in their partnership, Vivien Thomas was the technical innovator who first executed the details of their procedure. Thomas was also said to have more surgical skill than Blalock. His delicate precision would be a model for a generation of surgeons, many of them now heads of surgery departments.

- As director of surgical laboratories at Johns Hopkins for over 30 years, Thomas' last research project was to mentor a young African American surgeon, Levi Watkins, Jr. With Thomas' help, Watkins developed the automatic implantable defibrillator, a device that has saved over 100,000 lives.

- Prior to the civil rights era of the 1960s, medical schools graduated doctors that were almost all male (93%) and white (97%). By 2007, trends had improved for women (49% of all medical students) and minorities as a whole (37%). However, African Americans were still underrepresented, making up only 7% of all medical students.

- Before his death in 1964, Blalock confessed to many his regrets about not supporting Thomas going to medical school. Encouraged by his many supporters at Johns Hopkins, Thomas wrote his memoir Partners of the Heart which was published just days after his death in 1985. Thomas' and Blalock's portraits are right next to each other in the lobby of the Blalock Building at Johns Hopkins Hospital.

Where to Learn More

BOOKS

- Thomas, Vivien. *Partners of the Heart.* University of Pennsylvania Press, 1997.

DOCUMENTARIES

- *American Experience – Partners of the Heart.* PBS, 2003.

WEBSITES

- Partners of the Heart: www.pbs.org/wgbh/amex/partners

Discussion Questions

1. If you could discover a medical breakthrough or miracle to cure any of the world's diseases, what would it be and why?

2. Thomas was able to become a medical expert and innovator without any formal medical education. What is something important that you have been able to learn outside of formal education?

3. How do you think Thomas felt when he was not allowed to set foot in certain areas of Johns Hopkins? When have you felt like you were an outsider to the established crowd?

4. What do you think it would be like to be the parent of a "Blue Baby" before the Blalock-Taussig shunt was developed? Have you ever imagined what it would be like to lose your child?

5. Do you think Thomas and Blalock had successful marriages? How would you describe the ideal marriage?

6. What did Blalock mean when he said you haven't really lived unless you have a lot to regret? What is something that you regret?

7. Thomas did his work for very little money and with no recognition until the end of his life. What would be important enough for you to do, even for pennies and if you knew it wouldn't be recognized?

8. Imagine that you are given a chance to make a speech near the end of your life. Who would you want to be there? What would you hope to talk about?

9. Do you think Vivien Thomas is a good role model for you? Why or why not?

10. Do you think Alfred Blalock is a good role model for you? Why or why not?

Hotel Rwanda (2005)

Rated PG-13 for violence, disturbing images,
and brief strong language
121 minutes

The Story of Paul Rusesabagina

This movie tells the story of a hotel manager who saves over a thousand
lives from the Rwandan Genocide. Unlike most movie violence
that excites and desensitizes audiences, the violence in the movie is
restrained and delivers an important message. Hotel Rwanda is also
a family story, as the Rusesabagina family must stick together as they
face the threats of the brutal killings surrounding them.

Beyond the Movie

- Paul Rusesabagina has been described as a modern day Oskar Schindler. Using their influence, charisma, and courage, both Rusesabagina and Schindler (who was portrayed in the Academy Award winning film Schindler's List) sheltered and saved over 1,200 people from genocide.

- The Rwandan Genocide resulted in the death of at least 800,000 in 100 days, the fastest rate of mass killings in the 20th century.

- The origins of the Rwandan Genocide were based in European colonialism and racism. The Belgian rulers of Rwanda believed the Tutsi were superior to the Hutu because they more closely resembled Caucasians. They issued ethnic identity cards to make the division clear and offered privileged positions and education only to the Tutsi. When Rwanda became an independent country in 1961, the majority Hutu took power and took revenge on the Tutsi. This ethnic fighting reached its peak in 1994 with the Rwandan Genocide.

- International policy in Rwanda was influenced by the Somolia incident of 1993. This was told in the movie Black Hawk Down, where 18 U.S. soldiers trying to capture a warlord were killed in an ambush of street fighting. One year later in Rwanda, United Nations soldiers came only to retrieve foreigners and left the Tutsi defenseless against the Hutu militia.

- After the conflicts subsided, Rusesabagina stayed in Rwanda for two more years, returning to his position as hotel manager at the Hotel Diplomat. He applied for asylum and moved to Belgium with his family when there were threats on his life.

- Following the success of Hotel Rwanda, Rusesabagina continued to fight for the Rwandan people, starting the Hotel Rwanda Rusesabagina Foundation. In 2005, he received the Presidential Medal of Freedom, the highest civilian award in the United States. His memoir, An Ordinary Man: an Autobiography, was published in 2006. In the DVD Extra, Return to Rwanda, Rusesabagina and his wife are shown visiting the hotel and sites of the genocide.

Where to Learn More

BOOKS

- Rusesabagina, Paul and Zoellner Tom. *An Ordinary Man: an Autobiography.* Viking, 2006.

- Gourevitch, Philip. *We Wish to Inform You That Tomorrow We Will Be Killed With Our Families: Stories from Rwanda.* Picador, 1999.

- Ilibagiza, Immaculee. *Left to Tell.* Hay House, 2006.

- Power, Samantha. *A Problem from Hell: America and the Age of Genocide.* Harper Perennial, 2003.

DOCUMENTARIES

- *Frontline: Ghosts of Rwanda.* PBS Paramount, 2004.

WEBSITES

- Hotel Rwanda Rusesabagina Foundation: www.HRRFoundation.org

Discussion Questions

1. Do you think it's possible that genocide could happen again? How about in the United States or Western Europe? Why or why not?

2. Of the many difficult scenes to watch in the movie, which was the most emotional for you to watch and why?

3. Consider the words of the cameraman (played by Joaquin Phoenix): "I think if people see this footage, they'll say 'Oh, my God, that's horrible.' And then they'll go on eating their dinners." What is the most "horrible" news footage you have ever seen? Did you consider taking any action?

4. Paul Rusesabagina first had to decide whether to flee to safety with his children or leave his Tutsi wife behind. Later he had to decide whether to stay behind with the hotel refugees and send his family ahead. Would you have made the same two choices in these circumstances? Why or why not?

5. When was a time that you felt singled out for being different or mistreated for no good reason?

6. When was a time that you defended someone who was being singled out or mistreated for no good reason?

7. How did the Rusesabagina family cope with their fears? What are some ways that you have coped with any of your fears?

8. When was a time that someone in your family was in danger of losing their life?

9. How do you think your family would have made it through what the Rusesabagina family faced?

10). Do you think Paul Rusesabagina is a good role model for you? Why or why not?

The Pursuit of Happyness (2006)

Rated PG-13 for some language
117 minutes

The Story of Chris Gardner

This movie portrays a man who is able to overcome homelessness
while taking care of his son and pursuing his dreams of becoming a stockbroker. As he shows the courage to follow his dream, he
also remains dedicated as a father, keeping what matters most at
the forefront. The Pursuit of Happyness opens up a discussion of
personal goals and family connection.

Beyond the Movie

- As an association producer, Chris Gardner was there for the entire filming of movie. He also makes an appearance, walking by his character and son's character just before the movie ends.

- In the DVD Extras, Gardner talks about the importance of breaking the cycle of parents not being committed to their children. Growing up, Gardner witnessed domestic violence from his step-dad. As in the similar memoir and movie, Antwone Fisher, he also lived for a time in foster care. Now Gardner is a national leader in promoting fathers and sits on the board of the National Fatherhood Initiative.

- After leaving the Navy, Gardner worked as a research assistant for a prominent heart surgeon. Much like Vivien Thomas in Something the Lord Made, Gardner learned how to perform surgical procedures and wanted to go to medical school, before he decided to become a stockbroker.

- Gardner went from being homeless at the age of 28 to a millionaire at 34. He became CEO of Christopher Gardner International Holdings with offices in New York, Chicago and San Francisco. Through connections with Nelson Mandela to provide jobs and investment to South Africa, Gardner's assets under his management may approach $1 billion.

- As a philanthropist, Gardner gave back to the Glide Memorial United Methodist Church where he and his son received shelter. Working with the Reverend Cecil Williams (who plays himself in the movie), Gardner helped bankroll a $50 million project to provide affordable housing in San Francisco.

- In 2006, Gardner wrote his memoir that would become a NY Times #1 bestseller and inspiration for the movie. Less than half the book covers the time-span of the movie. The rest includes the many obstacles Gardner overcame growing up and before he decided to become a stockbroker.

Where to Learn More

BOOKS

- Gardner, Chris and Troupe, Quincy. *The Pursuit of Happyness*. Harper Collins, 2006.

- Fisher, Antwone and Rivas, Mim. *Finding Fish*. Harper Torch, 2002.

WEBSITES

- www.ChrisGardnerMedia.com

- National Fatherhood Initiative. www.Fatherhood.org

Discussion Questions

1. The first thing Gardner bought when he became a millionaire was Michael Jordan's Ferrari. If you became a millionaire, what would be the first thing you would buy?

2. How do you think Chris Gardner felt dropping off his son at daycare? What memories do you have of being apart from your parents as a child?

3. What did Chris Gardner mean when he told his son that you have to protect your dreams? Do you have any dreams that you have protected?

4. Do you agree that stockbrokers are happy? What profession do you think would make you the happiest and why?

5. What natural abilities allowed Chris Gardner to be a stockbroker? What profession would best suit your natural abilities?

6. How did Christopher inspire his dad to be successful? For parents, how have your kids inspired you? For teens, how would your kids inspire you if you were a parent?

7. How do you think spirituality helped Gardner and the other homeless people staying at the Glide Memorial shelter? How has spirituality helped you in your life?

8. At what point do you think Chris Gardner had to show the most strength? At what point in your life have you shown the most strength?

9. At what moment in your life do you believe you were most happy?

10. Do you think Chris Gardner is a good role model for you? Why or why not?

Freedom Writers (2007)

Rated PG-13 for violent content, some thematic material, and language

123 minutes

The Story of Erin Gruwell and the Freedom Writers

In this movie, a teacher encourages a classroom of at-risk teens to come together by sharing their own personal stories of adversity. Through the story of Anne Frank, she also opens her students' minds to importance of tolerance and the price of discrimination. Freedom Writers should raise other issues for discussion as well, including anger, respect, creativity and the value of education.

Beyond the Movie

- The "Freedom Writers" were named after the "Freedom Riders," a term coined by James Farmer, Jr. for the bus trips he led with other civil rights activists in 1961 to protest racial segregation in the South. A teenage James Farmer, Jr. is portrayed in The Great Debaters.

- Erin Gruwell of Freedom Writers is not the first Los Angeles teacher to help minority students defy expectations and be portrayed in a movie. Jaime Escalante of the similar film Stand and Deliver did the same, as he helped his minority students pass the AP calculus at rates so high they were accused of cheating.

- In addition to Miep Gies, Gruwell also invited to her class Zlata Filipovic. Like Anne Frank, Filipovic wrote her own diary of survival as a teenager, Zlata's Diary: A Child's Life in Wartime Sarajevo. Zlata's diary (as well as Anne Frank's) was the inspiration for Gruwell's students to write their own diaries, which were collected and published in 1999 as The Freedom Writers Diary.

- All 150 of Gruwell's students at Woodrow Wilson High School were able to graduate and most went on to college. Many of them were able to pay for college with the profits they received as authors of the Freedom Writers Diary.

- Just before the opening of Freedom Writers, violence struck the cast as 18-year-old Armand Jones (the actor who played the character falsely accused of murder) was killed outside a restaurant. For teens all across the United States, violence can be an everyday risk. According to the Centers for Disease Control, in 2005, 6.5% of high school teens reported carrying a weapon to school in the past month and 7.9% reported being threatened or injured with a weapon.

- After teaching at Woodrow Wilson High School for 5 years, Gruwell went on to be a professor at California State University at Long Beach. Later she formed the Freedom Writers Foundation, dedicated to teaching other teachers about the methods of her classroom. In 2007, she published Touched with Your Heart: Lessons I Learned from the Freedom Writers. She is featured on two of the Freedom Writers DVD Extras.

Where to Learn More

BOOKS

- Freedom Writers. *The Freedom Writers Diary: How a Teacher and 150 Teens Used Writing to Change Themselves and the World Around Them.* Main Street Books, 1999.

- Gruwell, Erin. *Teach With Your Heart: Lessons I Learned from the Freedom Writers.* Broadway; Reprint edition, 2008.

- Frank, Anne. *Anne Frank: The Diary of a Young Girl.* Bantam, 1993.

- Filipovic, Zltata. *Zlata's Diary: A Child's Life in Wartime Sarajevo.* Penguin, 2006.

DOCUMENTARIES

- *Anne Frank Remembered* (1995). Sony Pictures, 2004.

WEBSITES

- www.FreedomWritersFoundation.org

Discussion Questions

1. What teacher has made the biggest difference in your life? How so?

2. Were you ever fearful of any violence in your school? What is the most violence you've ever seen at school?

3. Eva identified the various groups at Woodrow Wilson High School based on color: Little Cambodia, Wonderbread Land, The Ghetto, and South of the Border. Are groups in your school separated by race? How else are social groups separated at your school?

4. Do you think your school is a place of tolerance? Why or why not?

5. How did the students of Room 203 learn to cope with their anger? What are the best ways that you have learned to cope with your anger?

6. When have you had to work at getting the respect of others? How did you do it?

7. Have you ever used a journal or another way of expressing your emotions artistically? What are your best ways of getting your emotions out?

8. Do you think the stories of Anne Frank or Zlata Filipovich have anything to say to you, as they did to the Freedom Writers? How so?

9. Erin Gruwell was clearly touched when her dad finally complimented her as a teacher. What is the best compliment you've ever received?

10. Do you think Erin Gruwell is a good role model for you? Why or why not?

The Great Debaters (2008)

Rated PG-13 for depiction of strong thematic material including
  violence and disturbing images, and for language and brief sexuality
123 minutes

The Story of James Farmer, Jr. and Melvin Tolson

In this movie, a black c ollege debate team upsets the 1935 national
debate champions from Harvard University. In their story are the
seeds of the civil rights movement, including the winning debate by
a teen who would become one of the great leaders of the 1960s. In
addition to racism and civil disobedience, The Great Debaters also
raises issues of responsibility, education, and family conflict.

Beyond the Movie

- In 1935, before a crowd of 2200 people, James Farmer, Jr. and his teammates defeated the reigning national debate champions. But that team was the University of Southern California, not Harvard.

- In Tolson's era, debate was so popular it was more like a spectator sport. Though its popularity would fade, it came back in the 1980s with the Urban Debate Leagues. Targeting at-risk youth in large cities, the urban debate program became increasingly successful. By 2007, 37,000 students had participated, with 71-91% going on to college.

- After coaching the Wiley College debate team, Melvin Tolson went on to become a leading poet of his generation. He was a contemporary of Harlem Renaissance and also the poet laureate for Liberia. His three most famous works – Rendezvous With America (1944), Libretto for the Republic of Liberia (1953), and Harlem Gallery (1965) – were published in a 1999 anthology, Harlem Gallery.

- James Farmer, Jr. became one of the "Big 6" of the civil rights movement. He was most known for founding the Congress of Racial Equality (CORE) and leading the Freedom Riders that protested racial segregation in 1961. His memoir Lay Bare the Heart: An Autobiography of the Civil Rights Movement was published in 1998, a year before his death.

- As in the movie, and like Ghandi, Alice Paul, and Martin Luther King, Jr., Farmer was a strong believer in civil disobedience. On the day of Martin Luther King, Jr.'s "I have a dream" speech in 1963, Farmer was in jail for disrupting the peace.

- Like King, Farmer was opposed to the more extreme tactics of activists like Malcolm X. His debate skills from Wiley College would prove useful. After winning four separate debates against Malcolm X, Farmer would credit his old teacher: "Come off it, Malcolm. You can't win. You didn't come up under Tolson."

Where to Learn More

BOOKS

- Bausum, Ann. *Freedom Riders: John Lewis and Jim Zwerg on the Front Lines of the Civil Rights Movement.* National Geographic Children's Books, 2005.

Discussion Questions

1. On civil disobedience, would you prefer to debate for the affirmative or the negative? Why?

2. What is the most racist act you've ever witnessed?

3. How did spirituality influence the Farmer family? What role has spirituality played in your life?

4. Consider what James Farmer, Sr. told his son: "We do what we have to in order to do what we want." Do you have the right balance of doing what you "have to" and what you "want to"?

5. Have you ever had a teacher like Melvin Tolson? How do you respond to his teaching style? What style works best for you?

6. How does your family value education? What have been your most important educational goals?

7. How do you think the Farmers managed when Jr. got home at 1:30 in the morning? How do you think your family would best manage this situation?

8. When has your family done well in debate? Why were you successful?

9. Do you think James Farmer, Jr. is a good role model for you? Why or why not?

10. Do you think Melvin Tolson is a good role model for you? Why or why not?

There is a growing recognition among pediatricians and psychiatrists about the negative influence of media. More research has confirmed the association between youth violence and violence portrayed in the media. There is also increasing evidence of decreased school performance in children and teens with the greatest media consumption.

All this is confirmation of what parents have already known: Media is shaping the lives of their teens in increasingly negative ways. In a recent national survey, a significant majority of parents indicated their belief that today's media is making youth too materialistic (90%), use more vulgar language (90%), engage in sexual activity earlier (89%), and become more violent (85%).

What can parents do to overcome all these negative influences? The most important thing parents can do is to monitor their teen's media use. This is the only way for parents to take an active role in shaping the effects of media on their teen. Teens need parents who will set limits on media use. But just as important (or more) is the need to take the time to experience media with their teen. It is only by sharing media together with their teen that parents are able to understand and shape the influence of media on their family.

This book should make it routine for parents and teens to discuss media. Each family movie night should help parents and teens become more comfortable starting up a conversation after media time is over. These media discussions are critical to make the best of media. With good communication habits, parents can know what media is doing to their teen. At the same time, they can use media as a window of opportunity to understand and guide their teen.

Recommendations

- Keep media out of the bedrooms and know the latest media technology. This is the only way to know the extent of teen media use. It is also the only way to have enforceable rules about media.

- Come up with rules about media that parents and teens can stick to. Guidelines should include all electronic media, including television, video games, and Internet.

- Know the parental advisories on media but don't trust them. The best way to know if media is appropriate for teens is for parents to experience the media themselves.

- Make an agreement to have regular family media time. Take turns choosing what to watch (or play). Include as much of the family as possible, but give siblings the option of doing something else.

- Use family media time as an opportunity to discuss the media's influence. As in the family movie nights, parents should not use family media time as an excuse to give a lecture. By listening and (when necessary) agreeing to disagree, parents can have a greater influence by encouraging teens to think for themselves.

Suggested Media Discussion Questions

1. What do you think was the funniest/scariest or most exciting/ emotional part of this media?

2. Do you think the media was realistic? What was the most unrealistic part? How about the most realistic?

3. Do you know anyone who reminds you of one of the characters in the media? Do you see yourself in any of the characters?

4. The Pleasantville question: What do you think it would be like if you were transported into the world of this media? How would your actions change the outcome?

5. What choices did the characters in this media make that you wouldn't? Why?

6. What stereotypes are shown in this media?

7. Why do you think this media makes money on teens?

8. Do you think there is a take-home message from this media? Is it a positive or negative message? Or is it mixed?

9. As a parent (or if you were a parent), for what age do you think this media is appropriate?

10. Do you think the characters on this media are good or bad role models for you?

Index of Discussion Questions

Role Models (16):

A League of Their Own #10
October Sky #10
The Insider #9
The Insider #10
Erin Brockovich #10
Thirteen Days #10
Rabbit-Proof Fence #10
Iron Jawed Angels #10
Hotel Rwanda #10
Something the Lord Made #9
Something the Lord Made #10
The Pursuit of Happyness #10
Freedom Writers #8
Freedom Writers #10
The Great Debaters #9
The Great Debaters #10

Global Studies (14):

The Insider #1
The Insider #2
Erin Brockovich #1
Thirteen Days #1
Thirteen Days #2
Thirteen Days #7
Rabbit-Proof Fence # 1
Iron Jawed Angels #1
Iron Jawed Angels #2
Iron Jawed Angels #9
Hotel Rwanda #1
Hotel Rwanda #3
Something the Lord Made #1
The Great Debaters #1

Balancing Priorities (9):   A League of Their Own #3
                             October Sky #5
                             Erin Brockovich #6
                             Erin Brockovich #7
                             Iron Jawed Angels #5
                             Hotel Rwanda #4
                             Something the Lord Made #5
                             The Great Debaters #4

Conflict Resolution (9):   A League of Their Own # 7
                             Thirteen Days #4
                             Thirteen Days #6
                             Thirteen Days #7
                             Thirteen Days #8
                             Freedom Writers #6
                             The Great Debaters #7
                             The Great Debaters #8

Goals (9):   October Sky #1
                             October Sky #3
                             Something the Lord Made #7
                             Something the Lord Made #8
                             The Pursuit of Happyness #3
                             The Pursuit of Happyness #4
                             The Pursuit of Happyness #5
                             The Great Debaters #4
                             The Great Debaters #6

Emotions (8):   A League of Their Own (Crying) #8
                             Rabbit-Proof Fence (Grief) #6
                             Iron Jawed Angels (Guilt) #6
                             Hotel Rwanda #2
                             Hotel Rwanda (Fear) #7
                             The Pursuit of Happyness (Happy) #9
                             Freedom Writers (Anger) #5
                             Freedom Writers #7

Race/Discrimination (8):	A League of Their Own #2
	Rabbit-Proof Fence #1
	Hotel Rwanda #5
	Hotel Rwanda #6
	Something the Lord Made #3
	Freedom Writers #3
	Freedom Writers #4
	The Great Debaters #2

Strength in Adversity (7):	A League of Their Own #9
	October Sky #3
	Erin Brockovich #3
	Erin Brockovich #8
	Rabbit-Proof Fence #9
	Hotel Rwanda #9
	The Insider #6
	The Pursuit of Happyness #3

| Telling the Truth | The Insider #6 |
| | The Insider #7 |

Education (6):	October Sky #1
	October Sky #2
	Something the Lord Made #2
	Freedom Writers #1
	The Great Debaters #5
	The Great Debaters #6

Communication Style (6):	A League of Their Own #6
	Erin Brockovich #4
	Thirteen Days #4
	Thirteen Days #5

Family Separation (5):   Rabbit-Proof Fence #7
Rabbit-Proof Fence #8
Rabbit-Proof Fence #9
Hotel Rwanda #4
The Pursuit of Happyness #2

Rebellion (5):   Iron Jawed Angels #4
Iron Jawed Angels #7
Iron Jawed Angels #8
Iron Jawed Angels #9
The Great Debaters #1

Marriage/Dating (4):   A League of Their Own #3
October Sky #4
Iron Jawed Angels #5
Something the Lord Made #5

Appreciating Family (4):   October Sky #6
October Sky #7
October Sky #8
Erin Brockovich #7

Money (4):   The Insider #1
Erin Brockovich #1
Erin Brockovich #2
The Pursuit of Happyness #1

Existential (3):   Thirteen Days #9
Hotel Rwanda #8
Something the Lord Made #4

Spirituality (3):   Rabbit-Proof Fence #3
The Pursuit of Happyness #7
The Great Debaters #3

Being Recognized (3):   October Sky #9
    Something the Lord Made #8
    Freedom Writers #9

Gender (3):   A League of Their Own #2
    Iron Jawed Angels #1
    Iron Jawed Angels #3

Tobacco (3):   The Insider #1
    The Insider #2
    The Insider #3

Drugs (2):   The Insider #4
    The Insider #5

Sexuality (2):   A League of Their Own #4
    Erin Brockovich #5

Peer Pressure (2):   Thirteen Days #3
    Rabbit-Proof Fence #4

Regret (2):   Iron Jawed Angels #6
    Something the Lord Made #6

Beyond Civilization (2):   Rabbit-Proof Fence #2
    Rabbit-Proof Fence #5

Athletics (1):   A League of Their Own #1

Alcohol (1):   A League of Their Own #5

Sibling Rivalry (1):   A League of Their Own #7

Being Helped (1):   The Insider #8

How to Dress (1):   Erin Brockovich #5

Self-Confidence (1):   Erin Brockovich #9

Family Rituals (1):   Rabbit-Proof Fence #3

Inspired by Children (1):   The Pursuit of Happyness #6

Violence (1):   Freedom Writers #2

Cliques (1):   Freedom Writers #3

References

Introduction

- Cline, Foster and Fay, Jim. *Parenting Teens with Love and Logic*. Updated and Expanded Version. Pinion Press, 2006.

- Garrison, David. *The use of movies to facilitate family engagement in psychiatric hospitalization*. Journal of the American Academy of Child & Adolescent Psychiatry. 46(9):1218-21, 2007 Sep.

A League of Their Own (1992). Sony Pictures, 2004.

- *A League of Their Own – The Documentary* (1986). Sony Pictures, 1994.

- Aubrecht, Michael. *Jackie Mitchell: The Pride of the Yankees*. Baseball Almanac, Nov. 2003. http://www.baseball-almanac.com/articles/aubrecht8.shtml

- Blumenthal, Karen. *Let Me Play: The Story of Title IX: The Law That Changed The Future of Girls in America*. Atheneum, 2005.

- Johnson, Susan. *When Women Played Hardball*. Seal Press, 1994.

- Macy, Sue. *A Whole New Ball Game: The Story of the All-American Girls Professional Baseball League*. Puffin, 1995.

- Merron, Jeff. *Reel Life: "A League of Their Own."* ESPN Page 2: Closer Look. http://espn.go.com/page2/s/closer/020511.html

- The All-American Girls Professional Baseball League Official Website. www.aagpbl.org

October Sky (1999). Universal Studios, 2005.

- *Apollo 13* (1995). Universal Home Video, 2005.

- Hickam, Homer. *Rocket Boys*. Delta, 2000.

- Hickam, Homer. *The Coalwood Way*. Island Books; 1st Ed, 2001.

- Hickam, Homer. *Sky of Stone*. Dell, 2002.

- Hickam, Homer. *We Are Not Afraid*. We Are HCI, 2002.

- Hickam, Homer. *Back to the Moon*. Island Books, 2000.

- Hickam, Homer. *Red Helmet*. Thomas Nelson, 2008.

- www.HomerHickam.com

- *In the Shadow of the Moon* (2007). Velocity/Thinkfilm, 2008.

- Kennedy, John F. (1961-05-25). Special Message to the Congress on Urgent National Needs Page 4. John F. Kennedy Library. Retrieved on 2007-09-20.

- *The Right Stuff* (1983). Warner Home Video, 2003.

- Wolfe, Tom. *The Right Stuff*. Picador; Reprint Ed, 2008.

The Insider (1999). Walt Disney Video, 2000.

- Centers for Disease Control. Morbidity and Mortality Weekly Report, 2005. http://www.cdc.gov/tobacco/data_statistics/MMWR/2005/mm5425_highlights.htm

- *Death in the West* (1983). Pyramid Home Video, 1991.

- *Frontline: News War. The Complete Series.* PBS, 2007.

- www.JeffreyWigand.com

- King C 3rd. Siegel M. The Master Settlement Agreement with the tobacco industry and cigarette advertising in magazines. *New England Journal of Medicine.* 345(7):504-11, 2001 Aug. 16.

- National Survey on Drug Use and Health, 2006. http://www.oas.samhsa.gov/nsduh/2k6nsduh/2k6Results.pdf

- *Secrets Through the Smoke.* CDC, 2001.

- Schroeder SA. Tobacco control in the wake of the 1998 master settlement agreement. *New England Journal of Medicine.* 350(3):293-301, 2004.

- *Secrets Through the Smoke.* CDC, 2001.

- *Thank You For Smoking.* Fox Searchlight Pictures, 2006.

- www.thetruth.com

- www.tobacoofreekids.org

Erin Brockovich (2000). Universal Studios, 2000.

- *American Justice: The Erin Brockovich Story.* A and E Home Video, 2001.

- Brockovich, Erin and Eliot, Marc. *Take It From Me: Life's a Struggle But You Can Win.* McGraw-Hill, 2002.

- Brockovich, Erin. The Power of One, 2001. Speech on Commonwealthclub.org. http://www.commonwealthclub.org/archive/01/01-02brockovich-qa.html

- www.Brockovich.com

- Los Angeles Times, 2000. Brockovich's X-Husband and X-Boyfriend Arrested in Sting. http://www.brockovich.com/images/pdfs/news/times sting.pdf

- National Toxicology Program. Report on the Toxicity Studies of Sodium Dichromate Dihydrate. National Institute of Health, 2007.

- Scorecard – The Pollution Information Site: www.scorecard.org

Thirteen Days (2001). New Line Home Video, 2001.

- *American Experience: The Kennedys.* PBS DVD Video, 2003.

- *Bobby* (2006). The Weinstein Company, 2007.

- *JFK* (1991). Warner Home Video, 2003.

- Kennedy, Robert F. *Thirteen Days: A Memoir of the Cuban Missile Crisis.* W.W. Norton and Company, 1999.

- May, Ernest and Zelikow, Philip. *The Kennedy Tapes: Inside the White House During the Cuban Missile Crisis.* W.W. Norton and Company, 2002.

- Stern, Sheldon. *The Week the World Stood Still: Inside the Secret Cuban Missile Crisis.* Stanford University Press, 2004.

- *The Fog of War – Eleven Lessons From the Life of Robert S. McNamara.* Sony Pictures, 2004.

Rabbit-Proof Fence (2002). Miramax Home Entertainment, 2003.

- *Ancient Mysteries: Dreamtime of the Aborigines.* A and E Home Video, 1997.

- Arden, Harvey. *Dreamkeepers: A Spirit-Journey into Aboriginal Australia.* Harper Perennial, 1995.

- Human Rights and Equal Opportunity Commission (an Australian government human rights agency). www.hreoc.gov.au

- Human Rights and Equal Opportunity Commission. Bringing Them Home: The "Stolen Children" Report, 1997. http://www.hreoc.gov.au/social_justice/bth_report/index.html

- Pilkington, Doris. *Caprice: A stockman's daughter.* University of Queensland Press, 1990.

- Pilkington, Doris. *Follow the Rabbit-Proof Fence.* University of Queensland Press, 1996.

- Pilkington, Doris. *Under the Wintamarra Tree.* University of Queensland Press, 2002.

- Stephens, Tony. Daughter Dies With Her Story Still Incomplete. The Sydney Morning Herald. Jan 15, 2004. http://www.smh.com.au/articles/2004/01/14/1073877902433.html?from=storyhs

Iron Jawed Angels (2004). HBO Home Video, 2004.

- Alice Paul Institute: www.alicepaul.org

- Baker, Jean. *Sisters: The Lives of America's Suffragists*. Hill and Wang, 2006.

- Bausam, Ann. *With Courage and Cloth: Winning the Fight for a Women's Right to Vote*. National Geographic Children's Books, 2004.

- www.equalrightsamendment.org

- *Ghandi* (1982). Sony Pictures, 2007.

- *The Great Debaters* (2008). Weinstein Company, 2008.

- *Not for Ourselves Alone: The Story of Stanton and Anthony*. PBS Home Video, 1999.

- *One Woman, One Vote*. PBS Home Video, 1996.

Something the Lord Made (2004). HBO Home Video, 2005.

- *American Experience – Partners of the Heart*. PBS, 2003.

- *Association of American Medical Colleges*. http://www.aamc.org/data/facts/2007/enrllbyraceth0207.htm

- Brogan TV. Alferis GM. Has the time come to rename the Blalock-Taussig shunt? Pediatric Critical Care Medicine. 4(4):450-3, 2003.

- McCabe, Katie. Like Something the Lord Made. *Washingtonian Magazine*, 1989.

- Nickens HW. Ready TP. Petersdorf RG. Project 3000 by 2000. Racial and ethnic diversity in U.S. medical schools. *New England Journal of Medicine*. 331(7):472-6, 1994.

- Partners of the Heart: www.pbs.org/wgbh/amex/partners

- Thomas, Vivien. *Partners of the Heart*. University of Pennsylvania Press, 1997.

Hotel Rwanda (2005). MGM Video and DVD, 2005.

- *Black Hawk Down* (2002). Sony Pictures, 2002.

- *Frontline: Ghosts of Rwanda*. PBS Paramount, 2004.

- Hotel Rwanda Rusesabagina Foundation: www.HRRFoundation.org

- Gourevitch, Philip. *We Wish to Inform You That Tomorrow We Will be Killed With Our Families: Stories from Rwanda*. Picador, 1999.

- Ilibagiza, Immaculee. *Left to Tell*. Hay House, 2006.

- Power, Samantha. *A Problem from Hell: America and the Age of Genocide.* Harper Perennial, 2003.

- Rusesabagina, Paul and Zoellner Tom. *An Ordinary Man: an Autobiography.* Viking, 2006.

- *Schindler's List* (1993). Universal Studios, 2004.

The Pursuit of Happyness (2006). Sony Pictures, 2007.

- *Antwone Fisher* (2002). 20th Century Fox, 2003.

- Barber, Andrew. Christopher Gardner: An Inspiring True-to-Life Rags-to-Riches Story. *aTrader*, Dec 2006/Jan 2007. http://www.atrader.com/Christopher_Gardner.html

- www.ChrisGardnerMedica.com

- Gardner, Chris and Troupe, Quincy. *The Pursuit of Happyness.* Harper Collins, 2006.

- Fisher, Antwone and Rivas, Mim. *Finding Fish.* Harper Torch, 2002.

- National Fatherhood Initiative. www.Fatherhood.org

- *Something the Lord Made* (2004). HBO Home Video, 2005.

Freedom Writers (2007). Paramount, 2007.

- *Anne Frank Remembered* (1995). Sony Pictures, 2004.

- Centers for Disease Control. Youth Risky Behavior Survey, 2005. http://www.cdc.gov/HealthyYouth/yrbs/pdf/trends/2005_YRBS_Violence_School.pdf

- Filipovic, Zltata. *Zlata's Diary: A Child's Life in Wartime Sarajevo.* Penguin, 2006.

- Frank Anne. *Anne Frank: The Diary of a Young Girl.* Bantam, 1993.

- *Freedom Writers. The Freedom Writers Diary: How a Teacher and 150 Teens Used Writing to Change Themselves and the World Around Them.* Main Street Books, 1999.

- www.FreedomWritersFoundation.org

- *The Great Debaters* (2008). Weinstein Company, 2008.

- Gruwell, Erin. *Teach With Your Heart: Lessons I Learned from the Freedom Writers.* Broadway; Reprint edition, 2008.

- Salkin, Allen. Hard Epilogue to 'Freedom Writers': A Violent Death. *New York Times*, Jan. 2007.

- *Stand and Deliver* (1988). Warner Home Video, 1998.

The Great Debaters (2008). Weinstein Company, 2008.

- Bausum, Ann. *Freedom Riders: John Lewis and Jim Zwerg on the Front Lines of the Civil Rights Movement.* National Geographic Children's Books, 2005.

- Bell, Gail K. Tolson, Farmer Intertwined by Wiley Debate Team. Marschall-NewsMessenger.com, 2008.

- Farmer, James. *Lay Bare the Heart: An Autobiography of the Civil Rights Movement.* Texas Christian University Press, 1998.

- National Association for Urban Debate Leagues: www.NAUDL.org

- *Freedom Riders: The Children Shall Lead.* University of Mississippi, 2005.

- Scherman Tony. The Great Debaters. *American Legacy*, 1997.

- Severo, Richard. James Farmer, Civil Rights Giant in 50s and 60s. *New York Times*, July 1999.

- Tolson, Melvin and Nelson, Raymond. *"Harlem Gallery" and Other Poems of Melvin B. Tolson.* University of Virginia Press, 1999.

Making the Best of Media

- Borzekowski, DL and Robinson, TN. The remote, the mouse, and the no. 2 pencil: the household media environment and academic achievement among third grade students. *Archives of Pediatrics & Adolescent Medicine.* 159(7):607-13, July 2005.

- Browne KD and Hamilton-Giachritsis, C. The influence of violent media on children and adolescents: a public-health approach. *Lancet.* 365(9460):702-10, 2005 Feb 19-25.

- Common Sense Media. The 2003 Common Sense Media Poll of American Parents, May 2003. Commonsensemedia.org

- *Pleasantville* (1998). New Line Home Video, 2004.

About the Author

David Garrison, M.D. is a child and adolescent psychiatrist and Assistant Professor at the University of Rochester of Medical Center in Rochester, New York. He works on an adolescent inpatient psychiatry unit, where he has been prescribing movies for hospitalized teens and their families for the past six years. He is also the director of the Psychiatry Clerkship, the required clinical experience in psychiatry for all medical students. In addition to the Family Movie Night prescription, Dr. Garrison's other innovation is a narrative exercise where students write up a short life story and give it to their patient before they leave the hospital. In 2007 he was selected to be a Dean's Teaching Fellow and in 2008 was the faculty recipient of the Leonard Tow Humanism in Medicine Award. He lives in Rochester, New York with family.